When Now Is Not Now

Alastair Reid

*for Miriam
with pleasure
Alastair Reid
2006*

*Pablo Neruda
Absence & Presence
by me AR.*

THE
POETRY
TRUST

Published November 2006 by

The Poetry Trust
The Cut, 9 New Cut,
Halesworth, Suffolk IP19 8BY

www.thepoetrytrust.org

ISBN 0-9550910-1-2

After 1 January 2007
ISBN 978-0-9550910-1-2

Printed by Leiston Press, Leiston, Suffolk

Most of these poems are reprinted from
Weathering: Poems and Translations
(Canongate, 1978)

Contents

*It was one of those odd moments
when now isn't now.*

David Mitchell (Black Swan Green)

ICSYLF

Writing is the most portable of occupations; and since it has been my livelihood from the fifties on, I have taken full advantage of this portability and its accompanying freedom to live in a number of different countries, contexts, and languages, which in turn have intruded themselves into much of what I have written.

Living in different places means growing separate selves, learning other languages and ways of being, and looking at the world from differing vantage points, without ever quite belonging to any of them. The state of being a foreigner wherever I am has become second nature to me. It is a condition that sharpens the ear and eye, that keeps awareness on its toes, and that takes nothing for granted. It means also that, wherever I am, the ghosts of other places and other lives are hovering close.

My constant preoccupation has always been with language and languages, with human oddness and eccentricity, with villages and the agrarian round, and with what geographers call 'land-life relations'. I have written, too, in many different modes. Though I began as a poet, through a long association with The New Yorker, I wrote a variety of things for that magazine -- essays, reviews, stories, and many articles on miscellaneous subjects, besides poems and translations. I was drawn to translation through my friendships with many Latin American writers and my enthusiasm for their writings. As one of them once wrote to me: 'The best thing about literature is the friends it brings you.'

I have always been grateful to have come first to poetry, before going on to write prose and to translate, for it is through poems that one experiences language at its most thrilling, in their miraculous compressions of sound, sense, and shape, those occasional felicities that Cyril Connolly called 'unbreakable toys for the mind'.

Of translation, Octavio Paz once wrote: 'In writing an original poem we are translating the world, transmuting it. Everything we do is translation, and all translations are in a way creations. The poet is the universal translator.' I feel exactly that about writing, be it poetry or

5

prose. It is all a matter of translating wordless perceptions and insights into language, into words that will appropriately contain them. There is no clear point of arrival, no definitive version. There is only the endless business of looking for the right words and, sometimes, being lucky enough to find them.

Consequently, the one enduring oasis in my life has been my writing table, which I set up wherever I find myself. I quote the Cuban writer Guillermo Cabera Infante, whose writing I revere: 'There is an island of the present, and that is writing. That island is my eternal island, the only kingdom I really owe allegiance to, the only country I inhabit, the house I live in, the house of words, the country of writing, the kingdom of language.'

Alastair Reid
October 2006

for SWM, of course ...

A Lesson in Music

Play the tune again: but this time
with more regard for the movement at the source of it
and less attention to time. Time falls
curiously in the course of it.

Play the tune again: not watching
your fingering, but forgetting, letting flow
the sound till it surrounds you. Do not count
or even think. Let go.

Play the tune again: but try to be
nobody, nothing, as though the pace
of the sound were your heart beating, as though
the music were your face.

Play the tune again. It should be easier
to think less every time of the notes, of the measure.
It is all an arrangement of silence. Be silent, and then
play it for your pleasure.

Play the tune again; and this time, when it ends,
do not ask me what I think. Feel what is happening
strangely in the room as the sound glooms over
you, me, everything.

Now,
play the tune again.

Whithorn Manse

I knew it as Eden,
that lost walled garden,
past the green edge
of priory and village,
and, beyond it, the house,
withdrawn, white,
one window alight.

Returning, I wonder,
idly, uneasily,
what eyes from inside
look out now, not in,
as once mine did,
and what might grant me
a right of entry?

Is it never dead, then,
that need of an Eden?

Even this evening,
estranged by age,
I ogle that light
with a child's greed,
wistfully claiming
lost prerogatives
of homecoming.

Scotland

It was a day peculiar to this piece of the planet,
when larks rose on long thin strings of singing
and the air shifted with the shimmer of actual angels.
Greenness entered the body. The grasses
shivered with presences, and sunlight
stayed like a halo on hair and heather and hills.
Walking into town, I saw, in a radiant raincoat,
the woman from the fish-shop. 'What a day it is!'
cried I, like a sunstruck madman.
And what did she have to say for it?
Her brow grew bleak, her ancestors raged in their graves
as she spoke with their ancient misery:
'We'll pay for it, we'll pay for it, we'll pay for it.'

The Academy

I do not think of the academy
in the whirl of days. It does not change. I do.
The place hangs in my past like an engraving.
I went back once to lay a wreath on it,
and met discarded selves I scarcely knew.

It has a lingering aura, leather bindings,
a smell of varnish and formaldehyde,
a certain dusty holiness in the cloisters.
We used to race our horses on the sand
away from it, manes flying, breathing hard.

Trailing to the library of an afternoon,
we saw the ivy crawling underneath
the labyrinthine bars on the window ledges.
I remember the thin librarian's look of hate
as we left book holes in her shelves, like missing teeth.

On evenings doomed by bells, we felt the sea
creep up, we heard the temperamental gulls
wheeling in clouds about the kneeworn chapel.
They keened on the knifing wind like student souls.
Yet we would dent the stones with our own footfalls.

Students still populate the place, bright starlings,
their notebooks filled with scribbled parrot-answers
to questions they unravel every evening
in lamplit pools of spreading argument.
They slash the air with theory, like fencers.

Where is the small, damp-browed professor now?
Students have pushed him out to sea in a boat
of lecture-notes. Look, he bursts into flame!
How glorious a going for one whose words
had never struck a spark on the whale-road.

And you will find retainers at their posts,
wearing their suits of age, brass buttons, flannel,
patrolling lawns they crop with careful scissors.
They still will be in silver-haired attendance
to draw lines through our entries in the annals.

It is illusion, the academy.
In truth, the ideal talking-place to die.
Only the landscape keeps a sense of growing.
The towers are floating on a shifting sea.
You did not tell the truth there, nor did I.

Think of the process – moments becoming poems
which stiffen into books in the library,
and later, lectures, books about the books,
footnotes and dates, a stone obituary.
Do you wonder that I shun the academy?

It anticipates my dying, turns to stone
too quickly for my taste. It is a language
nobody speaks, refined to ritual:
the precise writing on the blackboard wall,
the drone of requiem in the lecture hall.

I do not think much of the academy
in the drift of days. It does not change. I do.
This poem will occupy the library
but I will not. I have not done with doing.
I did not know the truth there, nor did you.

The O-Filler

One noon in the library, I watched a man –
imagine! – filling in O's, a little, rumpled
nobody of a man, who licked his stub of pencil
and leaned over every O with a loving care,
shading it neatly, exactly to its edges
until the open pages
were pocked and dotted with solid O's, like towns
and capitals on a map. And yet, so peppered,
the book appeared inhabited and complete.

That whole afternoon, as the light outside softened
and the library groaned woodenly,
he worked and worked, his o-so-patient shading
descending like an eyelid over each open O
for page after page. Not once did he miss one,
or hover even a moment over an *a*
or an *e* or a *p* or a *g*. Only the O's –
oodles of O's, O's multitudinous, O's manifold,
O's italic and roman.
And what light on his crumpled face when he discovered
as I supposed – odd words like *zoo* and *ooze*,
polo, *oolong* and *odontology*!

Think now. In that limitless library,
all round the steep-shelved walls, bulging in their bindings,
books stood, waiting. Heaven knows how many
he had so far filled, but still there remained
uncountable volumes of O-laden prose, and odes
with inflated capital O's (in the manner of Shelley),
O-bearing Bibles and biographies,
even whole sections devoted to O alone,
all his for the filling. Glory, glory, glory!
How utterly open and endless the world must have seemed to him,
how round and ample! Think of it. A pencil
was all he needed. Life was one wide O.

And why, at the end of things, should O's not be closed
as eyes are? I envied him, for in my place
across the table from him, had I accomplished
anything as firm as he had, or as fruitful?
What could I show? A handful of scrawled lines,
an afternoon yawned and wondered away,
and a growing realization that in time
even my scribbled words would come
under his grubby thumb, and the blinds be drawn
on all my O's, with only this thought for comfort –
that when he comes to this poem, a proper joy
may amaze his wizened face and, O, a pure pleasure
make his relentless pencil quiver.

Once at Piertarvit

Once at Piertarvit,
one day in April,
the edge of spring,
with the air a-ripple
and sea like knitting,
as Avril and Ann
and Ian and I
walked in the wind
along the headland,
Ian threw an apple
high over Piertarvit.

Not a great throw,
you would say, if you'd seen it,
but good for Ian.
His body tautened,
his arm let go
like a flesh-and-bone bow,
and the hard brown apple
left over from autumn
flew up and up,
crossing our gaze,
from the cliff at Piertarvit.

Then all at once, horror
glanced off our eyes,
Ann's, mine, Avril's.
As the apple curved
in the stippled sky,
at the top of its arc,
it suddenly struck
the shape of a bird,
a gull that had glided
down from nowhere
above Piertarvit.

We imagined the thud
and the thin ribs breaking,
blood, and the bird
hurtling downwards.
No such thing.
The broad wings wavered
a moment only,
then air sustained them.
The gull glided on
while the apple fell
in the sea at Piertarvit.

Nobody spoke.
Nobody whistled.
In that one moment,
our world had shifted.
The four of us stood
stock-still with awe
till, breaking the spell,
Ian walked away
with a whirl in his head.
The whole sky curdled
over Piertarvit.

I followed slowly,
with Ann and Avril
trailing behind.
We had lost our lightness.
Even today,
old as I am,
I find it hard
to say, without wonder,
'Ian hit a bird
with an apple, in April,
once at Piertarvit.'

Stalemate

Shrill interruption
of children's voices
raised in the garden.
Two of them stand
face to face,
each in one hand
weighing a stone,
each on his own
rigid ground.

You drop your stone,
then I'll drop mine.
No, you first.
Put yours down.
But if I do,
you'll throw yours.
Promise I won't.
I don't believe you.
Cross your heart?
Cross my heart.

Easy to call
the children in
before blows fall,
but not to settle
the ruffled feel
the garden has
as they both echo
the endless bicker
of lovers and statesmen,
learnt so soon.

Who began it?
Now, no matter.
The air is taut
with accusation.
Despair falls
like a cold stone
crossing the heart.
How did it start?
A children's quarrel.
What is its end?
The death of love.
The doom of all.

Quarrels

I can feel a quarrel blowing up in your body,
as old salts can smell storms
which are still fretting under the horizon,
before your eyes have flashed their first alarms.

Whatever the reason, the reason is not the reason.
It's a weather. It's a wellhead about to blaze gas,
flaring up when you suddenly stumble over
an alien presence in your private space.

You face me, eyes slitted like a cat's.
I can feel your nails uncurling.
The tendons in your neck twang with anger.
Your face is liquid as it is in loving.

Marking how often you say 'always' and 'never',
I on my side grow icy, tall, and thin
until, with watching you, I forget to listen,
and am burned through and through with your high passion.

Face to face, like wrestlers or lovers,
we spit it out. Your words nip, like bites.
Your argument's a small, tenacious creature
I try to stomp on with great logical boots.

Dear angry one, let the boots and the skittering beast
chase wildly round the room like Tom and Jerry
or who and why. Let us withdraw and watch them,
but side by side, not nose to nose and wary.

That is the only way we'll disentangle
the quarrel from ourselves and switch it off.
Not face to face. The sparks of confrontation
too easily ignite a rage like love.

The he-with-her subsides, the I-with-you
looms into place. So we fold up the words
and, with a movement much like waking up,
we turn the weather down, and turn towards.

The Figures on the Frieze

Darkness wears off and, dawning into light,
they find themselves unmagically together.
He sees the stains of morning in her face.
She shivers, distant in his bitter weather.

Diminishing of legend sets him brooding.
Great goddess-figures conjured from his book
blur what he sees with bafflement of wishing.
Sulky, she feels his fierce, accusing look.

Familiar as her own, his body's landscape
seems harsh and dull to her habitual eyes.
Mystery leaves, and, mercilessly flying,
the blind fiends come, emboldened by her cries.

Avoiding simple reach of hand for hand
(which would surrender pride) by noon they stand
withdrawn from touch, reproachfully alone,
small in each other's eyes, tall in their own.

Wild with their misery, they entangle now
in baffling agonies of why and how.
Afternoon glimmers, and they wound anew,
flesh, nerve, bone, gristle in each other's view.

'What have you done to me?' From each proud heart,
new phantoms walk in the deceiving air.
As the light fails, each is consumed apart,
he by his ogre vision, she by her fire.

When night falls, out of a despair of daylight,
they strike the lying attitudes of love,
and through the perturbations of their bodies,
each feels the amazing, murderous legends move.

Where Truth Lies

Maps, once made,
leave the impression of a place gone dead.

Words, once said,
anchor the fevers in the head.

Vows, once taken,
fade in the shadows of a place forsaken.

Oh, understand
how the mind's landscape forms from shifting sand,

how where we are
is partly solid ground, part head-in-air,

a twilit zone
where changing flesh and changeless ghost are one,

and what is true
lies between you and the idea of you –

a friction,
restless, between the fact and the fiction.

Directions for a Map

Birds' eyes see almost this, a tiny island
odd as a footprint on a painted sea.
But maps set margins. Here, the land is measured,
changed to a flat, explicit world of names.

Crossing the threads of roads to nibbled coastlines,
the rivers run in veins that crack the surface.
Mountains are dark like hair, and here and there
lakes gape like moth holes with the sea showing through.

Between the seaports stutter dotted shiplines,
crossing designs of latitude and language.
The towns are flying names. The sea is titled.
A compass crowns the corner like a seal.

Distance is spelt in alphabets and numbers.
Arrows occur at intervals of inches.
There are no signs for love or trouble, only
dots for a village and a cross for churches.

Here space is free for once from time and weather.
The sea has paused. To plot is possible.
Given detachment and a careful angle,
all destinations are predictable.

And given, too, the confidence of distance,
strangers may take a hundred mural journeys.
For once the paths are permanent, the colours
outlast the seasons and the deaths of friends.

And even though, on any printed landscape,
directions never tell you where to go,
maps are an evening comfort to the traveller –
a pencil line will quickly take him home.

The Spiral

The seasons of this year are in my luggage.
Now, lifting the last picture from the wall,
I close the eyes of the room. Each footfall
clatters on the bareness of the stair.
The family ghosts fade in the hanging air.
Mirrors reflect the silence. There is no message.
I wait in the still hall for a car to come.
Behind, the house will dwindle to a name.

Places, addresses, faces left behind.
The present is a devious wind
obliterating days and promises.
Tomorrow is a tinker's guess.
Marooned in cities, dreaming of greenness,
or dazed by journeys, dreading to arrive –
change, change is where I live.

For possibility,
I choose to leave behind
each language, each country.
Will this place be an end,
or will there be one other,
truer, rarer?

Often now, in dream,
abandoned landscapes come,
figuring a constant theme:
Have you left us behind?
What have you still to find?

Across the spiral distance,
through time and turbulence,
the rooted self in me
maps out its true country.

And, as my father found
his own small weathered island,
so will I come to ground

where that small man, my son,
can put his years on.

For him, too, time will turn.

Daedalus

My son has birds in his head.

I know them now. I catch
the pitch of their calls, their shrill
cacophonies, their chitterings, their coos.
They hover behind his eyes and come to rest
on a branch, on a book, grow still,
claws curled, wings furled.
His is a bird world.

I learn the flutter of his moods,
his moments of swoop and soar.
From the ground I feel him try
the limits of the air –
sudden lift, sudden terror –
and move in time to cradle
his quivering, feathered fear.

At evening, in the tower,
I see him to sleep and see
the hooding-over of eyes,
the slow folding of wings.
I wake to his morning twitterings,
to the *croomb* of his becoming.

He chooses his selves – wren, hawk,
swallow or owl – to explore
the trees and rooftops of his heady wishing.
Tomtit, birdwit.
Am I to call him down, to give him
a grounding, teach him gravity?
Gently, gently.
Time tells us what we weigh, and soon enough
his feet will reach the ground.
Age, like a cage, will enclose him.
So the wise men said.

My son has birds in his head.

Growing, Flying, Happening

Say the soft bird's name, but do not be surprised
to see it fall
headlong, struck skyless, into its pigeonhole –
columba palumbus and you have it dead,
wedged, neat, unwinged in your head.

That that black-backed tatter-winged thing
straking the harbour water and then plummeting
down, to come up, sleek head-a-cock,
a minted herring shining in its beak,
is a *guillemot*, is neither here nor there
in the amazement of its rising,
wings slicing the stiff salt air.

That of that spindling spear-leaved plant,
wearing the palest purple umbel,
many-headed, blue-tinted, stilt-stalked
at the stream-edge, one should say briefly
angelica, is by-the-way (though grant
the name itself to be beautiful).
Grant too that any name
makes its own music, that *bryony, sally-my-handsome*
burst at their sound into flower,
and that *falcon* and *phalarope* fly off in the ear,
still,
names are for saying at home.

The point is seeing – the grace
beyond recognition, the ways
of the bird rising, unnamed, unknown,
beyond the range of language, beyond its noun.
Eyes open on growing, flying, happening,
and go on opening. Manifold, the world
dawns on unrecognizing, realizing eyes.
Amazement is the thing.
Not love, but the astonishment of loving.

Curiosity

may have killed the cat. More likely,
the cat was just unlucky, or else curious
to see what death was like, having no cause
 to go on licking paws, or fathering
litter on litter of kittens, predictably.

Nevertheless, to be curious
is dangerous enough. To distrust
what is always said, what seems,
to ask odd questions, interfere in dreams,
smell rats, leave home, have hunches,
does not endear cats to those doggy circles
where well-smelt baskets, suitable wives, good lunches
are the order of things, and where prevails
much wagging of incurious heads and tails.

Face it. Curiosity
will not cause us to die –
only lack of it will.
Never to want to see
the other side of the hill
or that improbable country
 where living is an idyll
(although a probable hell)
would kill us all.
Only the curious
have if they live a tale
worth telling at all.

Dogs say cats love too much, are irresponsible,
are dangerous, marry too many wives,
desert their children, chill all dinner tables
with tales of their nine lives.
Well, they are lucky. Let them be
nine-lived and contradictory,
curious enough to change, prepared to pay
the cat-price, which is to die

and die again and again,
each time with no less pain.
A cat-minority of one
is all that can be counted on
to tell the truth; and what cats have to tell
on each return from hell
is this: that dying is what the living do,
that dying is what the loving do,
and that dead dogs are those who never know
that dying is what, to live, each has to do.

My Father, Dying

At summer's succulent end,
the house is green-stained.
I reach for my father's hand

and study his ancient nails.
Feeble-bodied, yet at intervals
a sweetness appears and prevails.

The heavy-scented night
seems to get at his throat.
It is as if the dark coughed.

In the other rooms of the house,
the furniture stands mumchance.
Age has graved his face.

Cradling his wagged-out chin,
I shave him, feeling bone
stretching the waxed skin.

By his bed, the newspaper lies furled.
He has grown too old
to unfold the world,

which has dwindled to the size of a sheet.
His room has a stillness to it.
I do not call it waiting, but I wait,

anxious in the dark, to see if
the butterfly of his breath
has fluttered clear of death.

There is so much might be said,
dear old man, before I find you dead;
but we have become too separate

now in human time
to unravel all the interim
as your memory goes numb.

But there is no need for you to tell –
no words, no wise counsel,
no talk of dying well.

We have become mostly hands
and voices in your understanding.
The whole household is pending.

I am not ready
to be without your frail and wasted body,
your miscellaneous mind-way,

the faltering vein of your life.
Each evening, I am loth
to leave you to your death.

Nor will I dwell on
the endless, cumulative question
I ask, being your son.

But on any one
of these nights soon,
the dark for you will not crack with dawn,

and then I will begin
with you that hesitant conversation
going on and on and on.

Weathering

I am old enough now for a tree
once planted, knee high, to have grown to be
twenty times me,

and to have seen babies marry, and heroes grow deaf –
but that's enough meaning-of-life.
It's living through time we ought to be connoisseurs of.

From wearing a face all this time, I am made aware
of the maps faces are, of the inside wear and tear.
I take to faces that have come far.

In my father's carved face, the bright eye
he sometimes would look out of, seeing a long way
through all the tree-rings of his history.

I am awed by how things weather: an oak mantel
in the house in Spain, fingered to a sheen,
the marks of hands leaned into the lintel,

the tokens in the drawer I sometimes touch –
a crystal lived-in on a trip, the watch
my father's wrist wore to a thin gold sandwich.

It is an equilibrium
that breasts the cresting seasons but still stays calm
and keeps warm. It deserves a good name.

Weathering. Patina, gloss, and whorl.
The trunk of the almond tree, gnarled but still fruitful.
Weathering is what I would like to do well.